met

MW00423599

metamorphosis

vincetta

dedication

to my mother
to my father
to my sisters
to my nephews
to my niece

who I believe I chose and who have taught me
so much about this journey we call life

gratitude

to all who I have crossed paths with across the
span of my life—leaving your imprint on me

to the authors of all the books I have read—
teaching me firsthand the importance and impact
of writing, language, and storytelling

to God, divine consciousness, primordial energy for expressing
itself through me and for guiding me to this very moment

table of contents

chapter one

caterpillar:
the foundation

part one

what was given

we are born
pure
clear
channels
of God

my entire childhood
I had
no idea of stability
no sense of normality

waking up
walking into
the apartment
each day after school

I didn't know
if my mother would be
angry and destructive
or kind and nurturing

I didn't know
if we would have food to eat
or working electricity

every day
every moment
I was on edge

life became
a guessing game
an unpleasant surprise
lingering around every corner

and so
I began to create
my own sense of
stability and normality
by trying to control

and give meaning to
what I could
grades
cleanliness
image

this coping mechanism
would manifest into
unrealistic
unhealthy
unauthentic
ways of being
and relating
to all around me

but first
it served me
helped me
to survive
to make it through
seemingly unscathed

there were times we couldn't afford to do laundry
washing our clothes with dish soap in the tub
there were times we couldn't afford a meal
surviving off of loaves of bread alone
my reality focused on just getting by
this is how survival mode was implanted
deep into my mind

I was on a spiritual journey
long before I had a clue
about spirituality

as a child
I had many moments
of crying my soul out
pleading with God
for support
for guidance
for some sense of relief
not being able to bear
the pain of it all
the emotional abuse
the physical abuse
the circumstances
of my incarnation

all of those times
led me to God
led me to my guides

I relinquished
all of my worries to them
and prayed for solace

I was told
to trust
trust that better was coming
trust that all that was happening
all the burden I was bearing
would serve a greater purpose

I felt alone
like an alien on Earth
within my family
within my community

I felt misunderstood
unable to relate

I felt invisible
never quite being
truly seen

I learned
to bury
my voice
my expression
my needs

I learned
they did not matter
there was no room for them
I had to be strong
        to hold space
for everyone else

my entire life
was a facade
of me appearing put together
on the outside
but slowly crumbling apart
on the inside

not wanting to be
any different
than I already was
I told everyone
to call me Ashley
my middle name

with shame
I hid my first name
a young Vincetta
just wanting to blend in
so badly
a pattern of shrinking
to belong
already being formed

I did not have
overwhelming support
a cheerleader in my corner
egging me on
pushing me forward
being the fuel
to the fire of my abilities

I took this personally
I thought it meant
that I was not good enough
that I was not worthy
of celebration
of invested attention
of love

thank you to all the friends
throughout those years
you were a saving grace
a heaven for me
in what seemed like
a living hell

we moved more times
than I can remember
for so many reasons
I cannot account for

this made it hard for me
to connect
to others
not seeing the purpose
if one day
the connection
could just be snatched away

the summer before eighth grade
I was thirteen
we were homeless
sleeping
from couch to couch
in the car
finally
in a shelter

my menstrual cycle started
it was a whirlwind for me
everything was
shifting
changing

so quickly

internally
externally

more loss of control
more leaning on God

suicide
death
the allure of it
being better than this life
has plagued my family
the pain
and the trauma
eating us alive

I've had to witness
my mom
passed out
overdosed
body almost
lifeless

I've sat
on the other side
of the phone
hundreds of miles away
as my sister called
to say
her final goodbyes
as she prepared
to overdose

I am still
eternally grateful
God had other plans
for them
for us

I myself
have even flirted
with the idea
many times
never fully choosing
to go through with it
cutting myself instead
heavily during high school

sometimes the pain
weighs too heavy
and we start to believe
pain is all there is
and all that there will ever be
and so we try and escape it
sometimes permanently

I went big chunks of time
years upon years
without speaking to
without seeing
my father

I never really
thought twice about it
growing up
it was normal
our fathers were
just imaginative characters
in the stories of our lives

but as I matured
I was able to accept
how this had left me
at my core
unsure of myself
a piece of who I was
had been missing
a hollow hole
unfilled

the energy
of the masculine
obscured
distorted
contaminated
and this
laid the foundation
for my interaction
with many men to come

undiagnosed bipolar
abuse to me
abuse to us
abuse to yourself

war zone
no love
all fear

taking in
taking on
all of your stress
            emotions
            troubles
all the while
mine were neglected

raising you
raising my sisters
raising myself

-mother wound

I bore witness
to your trauma
tormenting you
slowly inhabiting
your being
like the ultimate parasite

I became
the product of it

it multiplied itself
it leeched onto me

it did not realize
that I would be the one
to eat it alive

through all the suffering
the Earth gave me hope

warm winters
scorching summers

this is the environment
in which I bloomed

perspiration and baking
underneath the life-giving Sun

-flor(ida)

my mother is in me

in the way my feet
look like a melanated
replica of hers

on the tip of my tongue
as her accent faintly lingers
behind my every word
especially when I'm tipsy
and my tongue seems to get
too lazy to put up a fight

in the way that
                    words
                    thoughts
                    feelings
ooze out of me
into the form of poems

in the way that
the bold spirit
of passion and courage
radiate from this petite
human body

in my spirits inclination
to overcome
to push forward

in my connection
to the world not seen
and how that belief

was a seed planted
before me

-my mother gave me beauty

my father is in me

in my jaw
in my cheeks
in my lips

in the melanin
that allows me
to absorb the Sun
to become one
with the light

in the way he
instilled in me
the drive
to aim for more
to tap into my genius
to own my power

-my father gave me beauty

I grew up
the eldest
of three

feeling the pressure
to raise
guide
mentor

from a young age
my responsibility
was clear

even though
figuring out life
for myself
with no guidance
while supporting my sisters
on their journeys
has been a lot to bear

my most fulfilling role
has been nurturing them
my greatest teachers
have been them

I believe
we chose each other
in this lifetime
and I can only hope
that when all is said and done
we will have reverence
in that knowing

part two

what was multiplied

abuse has a way
of shrinking you
disconnecting you
from yourself
and the world around you

so it makes sense
that when he betrayed me
when he left bruises
on my body
in my own inability
to grasp the reality
I spiraled into the depths
of my own being
crawled into a shell
diminished my essence

unsure of how to deal
with the damage done
unable to accept
what had become

love and abuse
cannot coexist

for how could you
harm someone
consciously bring them
pain and anguish

and
in the same breath
proclaim
your care and love

that is a lie
the greatest manipulation

I allowed someone's demons
to swallow me whole
they viciously
took a hold of me
broke me down
and I let them

I didn't understand
what love really was
for how could I
eighteen years of my life
had been the blueprint

so I stayed
I made space
even after
I saw your own
self-hate

I tried to
love it out of you
how naive of me
to think
that I could love
someone enough
to make them love
themselves

so I stayed
I made space
even after
you killed off
a part of me

I left the door open
for understanding
and compassion
yet what was there
to understand

you had violated me
beyond belief
yet I thought
you could still love me

I hope you learn
not to treat women so recklessly

I hope you learn
to value their divinity

even if we never make amends
I hope you never do this again

my dreams deceive me

they speak of
love and emotion
that warm my body
and ignite me
from the inside out

they show me
happiness and connection
to a beautiful soul

they deceive me
because I awake alone
with a heart full of stone

energy transfers
at the speed of light
the channel shifts
we align like stars
in the midnight sky

you were
like a cool breeze
on a hot summer day

like a rain shower
after weeks of drought

like the first sight of greenery
after the long winter months

you gave me hope
that what I needed
was always
right around the corner

do you think
that we were both
emitting a frequency
that brought us to each other
like birds in the dawn of day
singing our songs to one another

my mirror
you amplified
the worst parts of me
so I could see
where the changes
still needed to be

my mirror
you amplified
the best parts of me
so I could see
the Godliness
inside of me

as the honeymoon phase
fades away
it leaves us
in a haze
suspended above
the ground of reality
yet hundreds of feet down
from cloud nine

I tried so hard
but it wasn't enough
if only you knew
how hard it was for me
to open up to you

maybe then
you would have appreciated
the stems that sprouted
from my lips
as clues
of what could blossom

maybe then
you would have learned
to water the words
that tried their best
to push through
the rigid ground

you shrunk me
again
made me feel
worthless
small
inferior

all the things
I know
I am not
yet still
I feel

disrespect
neglect
of my
essence
heart
being
logic
continuously
going round
and round

but now
I must swallow
my sorrow
for you have decided
it's time to be serious
and for me
to let all the hurt go
all for the simple fact
that you said so

my heart is bruised
wounded
still recovering
from the last time
you mishandled her

she's healing
and afraid
that if she lets you in
you'll do it again

she's weary of you
the things you say
the things you do

she loves you
but she's not quite sure
you love her too

I live on edge
in doubt
of my own words
            actions
            being

not knowing
what will trigger you
to choose
that you
no longer love me

that I am somehow
no longer worthy

you come back
I let you in
with no
hesitation

you take it
for granted
you think
you'll always
have access to me

I guess
there's no one
to blame
but me

I taught you
how to treat me
by letting you
back in
so easily

I'm tired of
being used
picked up
then thrown aside
living at the whim
of someone else's
mood swings

it's no way to live
it's no way to love

it is becoming impossible
to fully commit to someone
who doesn't commit to
anyone or anything
but themselves

it's not healthy
for someone like me
to love someone like him
because I will give
and give
and give
and he will take
and take
and take

I will always feel unloved
and he will never understand
why giving the bare minimum
just isn't enough
and why a woman like me
won't settle for crumbs

coming
going
staying
turning
away
from each other
from ourselves

in moments
we are together
connected forever
even when
in time
we are no longer
existing as one

there is a part of me
you will forever have

a part that
I can never get back

a part that
I had to let go

a part that
wasn't the me
I am truly supposed to be

my heart is still sad you know
she can't let go sometimes
even though
my mind has moved on
and my legs have moved forward

my heart still hopes
that one day you'll return
and you would have changed
but the best parts of you
would have stayed

and my heart will sigh with relief
that she knew it was you all along

heartbreak
comes in waves
of despair
of hope
of strength
of longing
of grieving
someone who is
alive and well
but dead to you

letting you go
has been both
the best and worst
times of my life

when I first met you
I felt the urge
to push you away
to run
as fast as I could

and
I felt the urge
to get closer
to allow it all
to unfold

which was right
I may never know
for loving you
has brought me
great ecstasy and joy
yet much torment and sorrow

you were my twin flame
and you burned me alive

I want you to know
letting you go
wasn't easy
walking away
closing that door
left me weak to my knees

my heart
wondering where you went
my hands
grasping for you
and realizing you were gone
shattered me
tears washed through me
like rapid rivers
hoping
you'd appear to catch them

but you were gone
and it occurred to me
that I had to pick myself up
and move on

for a brief moment
we felt each other's intensity
and became engulfed
in the magnetic pull
of our energy fields

not knowing
that it was just a moment
and we would continue
on our separate orbits
eternally changed
by one another
but one without the other

I mourned for you
for hours I cried
hours that turned to days
that turned to weeks
that turned to months

I cried through years of us
I cried until it felt like
I had cried you out of me
was that possible
that one day my eyes were dry
and I was lifetimes away from you

where do feelings go to die?

maybe you were
just a lesson
that I tried to
turn into a thesis

just a moment
that I tried to
turn into eternity

today is the day
I pledge to
no longer seek you
no longer look to
complete you

today is the day
I pledge to
no longer leave space
for you to take
in my mind
in my heart
in my energy field
I take it all back
I redeem it
and declare it mine

I realized
I was not afraid
to lose you
and I knew
in that moment
that if I was truly willing
to lose you
I was willing to lose
a part of myself
willing to face
a death
a loss
of all I've known
to surrender blindly
to the current of life
a level of liberation
I had never known

all of my romantic relationships
up to this point
have been
shallow
a show
an illusion of care

both of us unhealed
trying to fill a void
and have one filled

though the love wasn't real
I took beautiful lessons
teachings of passion
        courage
        unconditionality
that will live forever within me

through all the pain you caused me
I still want to thank you
for the inspiration that grew
and the awakening that blossomed
from the cracks of our foundation

for teaching me subliminally
the beautiful balance
of strength and softness
of death and rebirth

blue for you
for your home
for your wounds
for your heart

for my chakra
for my lesson
for my healing
blue for me too

-lolu

maybe my heart knew
you would be the one
to bring me back home to myself

-the day we met, my heart leapt out my chest

you awakened
something in me
that needed to be
released
set free

allowed to be
seen
heard
felt
naturally

you awakened
my divine femininity

the universe knew
I had trouble letting go
my loyalty had turned
to a fault
I was unable to separate
who you were
from the idea of
who you could be

so it brought me
back to you
me having evolved
            healed
            mended myself
and you
having missed this part
of my journey
of my growth
of my unfolding

so we met again
both different
yet the same
and you showed me
unknowingly
that I had to let go

because if you
could not recognize
            honor
            value
the beautiful transformation
of who I am now

then how could you appreciate
who I would become

time has passed
and time has gone
it's about time
for me to move on

chapter two

cocoon:
into the void

I was strong
for so long
I became weak

it lingers you know
no matter how many
loves
laughs
lives
seem to pass you by
the pain
is still there
hidden
waiting
to expose
all that you thought
no longer mattered

I live in a fog
my vision clouded
by all that has happened
I am unable
to see my way out

I am tired
of these dark clouds
hanging above me
following me
smothering me

I can't breathe
        speak
        see
the same

please rain
please pour
please storm

so that the clouds
can finally part

how do I heal
break free
break chains
that tie me down

I try to get
up
out
away
but it's in me
my bones
my blood
my breath

driver's seat
hijacked
emotions
take over
logic
cannot connect
reroute is not
successful

seeking confirmation
      worthiness
      acceptance
from everywhere
but here

unhealthy attachment
clinging
grasping
for validation
for love
for all the things
I should be giving myself

ain't it a shame
that I keep playing
these games
weaving in and out
of realizing my potential
and suffocating it

I am my biggest enemy
my largest blockade

I stand tall and wide
in the doorway
of growth
of evolvement
of flow

I look myself in the eyes
and say
it's too late
you're not enough

I whisper in my ears
the lies
that hold no truth
the doubt and uncertainty
that eat away at my joy

I surround myself
with the life-draining stench
of fear

I paralyze myself
with what ifs
and worst-case scenarios

who is getting in my way
it is I

fear
projection
hiding
preparing
controlling
of the unknown
of the future
of the past

in the now
waiting
feeling
knowing
that it will come
to pass

learning
as I emit
it manifests
self-fulfilling
prophecy
be careful

trying not to drown
can you feel me
gasping for air
my hands reaching
for something
tangible
solid
real

lost
found

ebbs
flows

it comes
then it goes

in between
being truly seen
and being utterly
misunderstood

am I not enough
in the way
I'm not
just like you

it seems
all they do
is babble on
in Babylon

-disconnected

feeling heavy
weighed down
by the energetic burdens
of this world
dense
hard
restrictive

these feelings
closer
than they need to be
but they are here
and I am with them
acknowledging them
them acknowledging me
calling them out
letting them leave

realizing
I have no place
for them here
they cannot
make a home out of me
not even an airbnb
they must leave
almost as quickly
as they came
like a rough wind
shaking up a tree
but only momentarily

I feel everything
so deeply
the slightest perceiving
of injustice
and I am ready
to rage a war
my empathy
connecting me
to the troubles and joys
of the collective consciousness

at any moment
a million rivers
can come pouring
out of me
like my heart
can break itself in two
and put itself back together
for you

I wanted to
outrun the darkness
outsmart the monsters

I believed it was possible
to be free from the pain
if I locked it away
pushed it down
to the deepest parts
of my mind
of my being

but it found its way out
I couldn't ignore it
its energy
devouring me
from the inside out

sometimes the truth
gets too scary
too intimidating
the emotions
    thoughts
     memories
     revelations
too overwhelming

and I run

I run
so my attention
can be filled
so that I do not
have to deal
with the undeniable
truth of it all

and for so long
I thought running
would work
but I only ended up
running back into
myself

suffocation
restriction
resistance

unable to surrender
to the flow of life
unable to trust
the natural unfolding
feeling betrayed
that life had previously
brought me to struggle
            to pain
            to heartbreak

wanting to avoid this
I assumed
a false sense
of control
that unraveled
into chaos

for I was beginning to create
the very thing
I was attempting to avoid

why do we
run in circles
running from
the very thing
we know will lead us
to exactly where
we wish to be

my mind would like me to think
I've hit a fork in the road
that I've ran face-first
into a brick wall

but my spirit knows
this is only a hurdle
one that shall be conquered
one that will serve its purpose
then cease to exist

I saw how avoiding my darkness
would only lead me to
a life of numbing and running
a never-ending cycle
of despair

so I made a choice
to face it all
no matter how ugly it got
no matter how much I felt
like I was losing my grip
on myself
on my reality

I was not going to let the illusions
run the show any longer

I was taking my power back

fear crept
and crept
and I wept

at first
feeling overwhelmed
then recognizing
I was the one
feeding the monster
so I decided
to starve it
to let it die

I held the power
I had pulled its card

cutting off
the bondage
of the past
mistakes
failing
heartbreak
anger

slashing
the chains
running fast
knowing that
I must go now
or it'll be too late

I lean into
the discomfort
I lean into
the resistance

I lean into
the years
of being rock hard
when really
I just wanted to be soft

my inner child
enraged
cried out
why was I not loved
why was I not enough

and I ran to her side
listened to her
cried with her
and began to shower her
with unconditional love

one of the biggest
lies I lived
was that I did not need
help
support
community

I was independent
I had it all figured out
I could do it all by myself
a story ingrained in me
a false truth
I pledged to honor
with every ounce
of my being

my ego has been
my biggest enemy
feeding me
illusions
narratives
Shakespearean plays

trying
so
damn
hard
to keep me
from witnessing
and accepting
the truth
of life
of this reality
of who I am

I did not know
healthy love
from another woman
my mother
myself

so how could I handle
any other woman
with love

many friendships died
I did not honor them
in love
in light
in truth

for all my life
I had been programmed
to believe
this narrative that you
were out to get me
jealousy
backstabbing
betrayal
had been planted
in my subconscious

I could not trust you
I could not love you

when I did not know
my own power
my own beauty
I felt jealousy
        anger
        resentment
toward women who did

not openly
but in my heart
it bubbled
showing me that
I needed to learn
to own
and understand
my power
my beauty
so that the power
and beauty
of others
would only add light
to my shine

making peace
with the idea
that my anxiety
is my friend
not my enemy
that I do not have to be
at war with my unease
that I can welcome it
with a warm hug
and understanding
comforting it
loving it
showing it
that it is safe
and it can be
whatever it needs to be

but eventually
I will have to set it free

rejection paralyzed me
that wound deep
within the root chakra
the need to belong
and never quite feeling
like I did

a confirmation of
my deepest fear

I had to learn
that I am not
nor will I ever be
for everyone

I had to learn
not to take things
so personally

the solution
I had to focus
on being enough for me

every time I suppressed
            distorted
            silenced myself
the distance between
my truth and my mask
grew further
and the influence of the mask
grew stronger
forming a life of its own
my truth fighting
            clawing
to regain the power
it had so easily handed over

there have been countless times
where I have overextended myself
                censored myself
                abandoned myself
for the sake of another

and what for?

for the temporary filling of a void
for the illusion of love
for the facade of belonging

fear of abandonment
fear of not being enough
fear of not belonging

made me stay in places
I had no business staying
made me say things
I had no business saying

fear is not the monster
that we swore
was in the closet
the one our parents
told us not to worry about
it is the one that haunts us
from inside our very own beings

there has been
so much
anger and shame
living inside of me

they've been there
brewing silently
exploding out of me
at times uncontrollably
            unexpectedly
rearing their heads
showing me their power
                their strength

begging me to
set them free
letting me know
they were tired of
living inside of me

perfectionism
has been a prison

scared to fail
when in reality
there was no failing
only falling
landing
and getting back up

scared to make a mistake
when in reality
there were none
to be made
only lessons to be learned
experiences to be had
life to be lived

I am not perfect
nor will I ever be
this false illusion
of an ideal

I will be
the highest
version of me
that is all
I wish to be

the more I begged
            pleaded
with family
with friends
with lovers
with you

to see me
to hear me
without projections
or false ideals

the clearer it became
that my inner child
was begging
the same from me
to be allowed to be
without the fear
            the insecurities
            the fantasies
            the judgements
to be allowed to be
me in all my glory

hearing you
admit your wrongdoings
admit you didn't keep me safe
admit you didn't give me love
healed me

crying with you
as you held me
my guards tumbling down
the resentment melting away
in your arms
in that moment
my inner child
finally feeling seen

hearing you apologize
so genuinely
freed me

-mami

the shadows
can swallow you whole
if you let them
if you stand by
and play victim

the shadows
can set you free
if you let them
if you allow yourself
to embrace them

the shadows
will only have the power
that you give them

for the shadows
are just another part
of you

burning all of it
to the ground
until all that remains
is a foundation
of soil
of Earth
that I will nurture
back to health
so that lasting life
can be built

spiraling
out of control
yet grounded
in ethereal knowing

I sat
I lied
down on my mat

I prayed to God
to help me
to give me
      courage
      faith
to face it all

I met myself
      my inner child
      my shadow
      my soul
      my heart
      my ego

we cried out decades of trauma and frustration
we laughed at the memories and the mistakes
we smiled at how far we'd come

we healed
in the dark

you must be patient with yourself
you cannot expect to heal
                    mend
                    resurrect
in a day
you are a kingdom
            universe
            empire
and those my dear
need time
that you must take

as I carry trauma
              karma
              dharma
              gifts
              abilities
              guilt
              shame
              freedom
              courage
              joy
from other lifetimes
from other bloodlines
I realize
not all I carry is mine
the gift and the curse
of inheritance

some days
some moments

I weave in and out
of grief
of disappointment
of anguish

of all
the mistakes
the struggles
the hardships

but I am learning
to shower these times
with love
      forgiveness
      grace

understanding
that it is okay
to experience
all these emotions
to deal with them
as they arise
knowing the key lies
in not allowing myself
to over-identify

questioning
examining
inspecting
my every thought
          feeling
          belief
that rifts
and shifts
that blocks off
the harmony
that restricts
the flow of life

for I know
that is a signal
a red flag of sorts
telling me to
take a closer look

go deeper
see the root
drop the illusions
see the fruit

✸ I was subconsciously controlled
by the ghosts
of my trauma
possessed
by the past

looking back
I wasted so much time
running from parts of me
not knowing
how to deal with it all
not wanting
to feed the energy
for fear
that it would consume me

when really
it just wanted
to be validated
to be understood
above all
to be freed

to be accepted
as part of me
as part of my journey

the story of the victim
a role I've played plenty
woe is me
God hates me
everyone is out
to get me

of course they are
for that is what
you are believing
you are creating
you are only the character
you choose to be
your life is only the story
you agree it to be

✳ speak
even if you
feel weak inside
from the endless
chatter of doubt
and fear

speak
for no other reason
than to be heard
you are worthy
of being listened to
of being considered

speak
so that you
become stronger
in your power
and confident
in your truth

speak
unblock
purify
your throat
chakra

activating
my energy
cultivating it
to transmute
all the pain
into power
into pleasure
into peace

create the space
to love
   cry
   laugh
   scream
yourself back to life

tears are
emotion
moving
flowing
morphing
into this
physical realm
finding their way
out of the body
freeing themselves

-cry

I cry nearly every day now
a daily ritual

of gratitude
for all that is
and all that shall be

of release
for all that has passed
and all that has served me

with my childhood
came trauma

what a marvelous
cosmic orchestration
that I ended up back here

that the universe
brought me back to the land
that energetically
held so much hurt
so that I could heal it all 🐚

I wonder
have I ever
known a home
moving
shifting
trying not
to be consumed
by the despairs
of single motherhood
minimum wage
same story
different day

I wonder
have I ever
known a home
will I ever
find my own
or has it been
inside me
all along
my body
my soul
being a shelter
        a retreat
of love

yoga changed my life
ever since that fated day
in high school
in an orange county library
body
breath
stillness
grounded

meditation changed my life
ever since that fated day
in college
in leon county florida a&m
body
breath
stillness
liberated

my life has been
undoubtedly guided
toward the path of enlightenment
attuned with ever-present
ancient truth

yoga
teaches me patience
teaches me trust
with my body
with my soul

allowing me to unite the two
in beautiful harmony
a mindful dance

alleviate your mind
       your soul
       your heart
       your body
from the baggage of the past
from the pain that no longer
serves a purpose in the present
from the fear of the unknown future

alleviate yourself
from all that is not
here and now

my identity shed
like a snake's skin
coming undone

parts of me
no longer fit
so they died
and though I was happy
to see them go
I grieved
for they were
a part of me

I was living
on the middle ground
of connection
and disconnection
death and rebirth

reframing
rebuilding
reconsidering
all that I was
all that I am

is it possible
to lead a new life
to begin anew
without any thoughts
or feelings
of what used to be
to wipe the slate clean
to fully let go
of all that no longer
truly exists

today
I was alive
I was present
I did my best
that is enough

me showing up
just being
just breathing
is enough

giving myself credit
for my strength
for my magic
for my ability
to keep reaching higher
even in the midst
of the abyss
even when the waves
of life's lows
try to swallow me whole

even though I have made mistakes
I release the shame and guilt
I choose forgiveness
I choose compassion
I choose unconditional love

I am free
to start again
to let go of it all
to begin a new life
and leave the old one
where it's left me

taking my time
strengthening the bond
between me and the universe
            me and love
            me and myself

allowing myself
to unravel
to discover
the wonder again

protecting myself
from all that takes me for granted
all that chooses
to bring me chaos over peace
is released

as I release
fear-based
ways of relating
        of thinking
        of being
more love
comes pouring
into my life

healing my heart
giving it permission
to truly feel
to let its guard down
to allow the flow of love
to give it freely
to receive it gratefully

healing my heart
to be love again

deep down
we all want
to be loved
     seen
     understood
by another
but that is where
the danger lies
wanting can lead
to desperation
to yearning
for something
for someone
outside of ourselves
to validate
all that we are

I have to be mine
for myself
before I am anyone else's

I have to have
my own reservoir of love
my own fountain of joy
to claim
before I try to take
from anyone else's

why do we settle for the story
that we will find love someday
when we can find love now
inside ourselves

one of the greatest lessons
moving forward
is to seek approval
        acceptance
        love
        support
from within

so no matter what happens
I will not be rocked
or swayed
or moved
by others
and their overflow
or lack of it

choosing me
I'm choosing me

these past few months
have been a realization
of a multitude of fears
that have lived inside me
coming undone

you are safe now

an affirmation
a reassurance
to myself
    my inner child
    my inner goddess

I am safe now

after so much is
       accepted
       learned
       reflected
       released
comes integration

the most overlooked
part of this journey
is granting yourself
time
grace
patience
needed to become

just as it's always been
you must graduate
from one level
before moving
to the next
you must pass
the test
before you proclaim
mastery

remember
it's easier to preach
than to practice
easier to say
than to do

but do not worry
you have it in you
you have arrived at this point
you have everything you need
to transcend it all

fear will not leave me
bare and dry
I will look it in the face
and laugh
at its attempt
to keep me petrified
of my own existence

I choose to let life
pour out of me
like a fire hydrate
bust wide open
a flood of expression
blasting forth
unstoppable
uncontrollable
and free

I thank you for giving me inspiration
even when it seemed impossible
you gave it to me
in mountains
in oceans
in an abundance
of trauma
of heartache
of lessons
of feelings and experiences
that manifested
into the most beautiful creations

I am the reset
I am where the struggle ends
I am where the miracles start

I am the alchemist
    the catalyst

I am where the energy
is finally transformed

sprouting
pushing past
the seemingly infinite
layers of dark cold soil
through what feels like
an all-encompassing force
swallowing me whole

up
up
up
towards the light
I wade my way through
then finally I feel
the warmth of the sun
the caress of the wind
I've emerged into a new life

chapter three

butterfly:
seeing with new eyes

my life has been a series
of trial and error
a grand experiment
in science
in spirituality
in the will of a soul

I look back now
and see
how parts of me
weren't me
just trauma
lingering
reaching
projecting
manifesting itself
into form
taking on a life
of its own

I was born into
total ignorance
the veil heavy

I have spent
my entire life
unconsciously
consciously
liberating myself

despite all the pain that came
so did beauty
      wisdom
      compassion
      grace
for you are only human
for you were only trying
your best

for everything that has happened
made me everything I am
for trusting it was all a part
of God's divine plan

no longer
allowing myself
to drown
in order for others
to float

what a revolution
me loving myself
fully and freely

self-love lies
just beyond
the acceptance
of your darkest truths
and the healing
of your deepest wounds

give yourself
everything you long for
shower yourself
with all you desire
for then no one can
threaten to destroy
the foundation of love
you have built
for yourself

I am
    all the power lies in me
I am
    accountable for my energy
I am
    God consciousness activating

you are a God of your universe
a creator and destroyer
of your world

you are where it all starts

you are a part of the alpha
and the alpha you are

we are a part of the one
and the one we are

we are not separate
we are connected
a mass energy existing

we are water
       earth
       air
       fire
       ether

we are a part
of all that is
  all that was
  all that ever will be
primordial energy

a piece
a link
the whole entire
universe

our minds
our abilities
are limitless
our expansion
innate
consciousness
naturally evolving
all we must do
is be open
surrender
trust
in the inherent
unfolding

we must let go
of all things
that trap us
in our human minds
in the illusion

we must let go
and see each moment
as it is
an endless
boundless
divine moment
of perfection

I know our brains
are purposely trained
to look at it all
through a negative lens
but try again
practice
viewing it all
with appreciation
with awe
for it is all
truly a miracle
we have been witnessing

love or fear
abundance or scarcity
where do you lie

there is no in between
you must pick a side

fear is like a boulder
that lingers over your head
threatening to drop
at any moment
crushing you
excruciatingly
to death
while all along
it is an illusion
a ball made of foam

in reality
not of any harm
to you
a threat
only in your thoughts

too much
        planning
        controlling

not enough
        attracting
        flowing

knowing and believing
are two different things

doing and allowing
are on two different ends

becoming
unattached
letting go
trusting in
the flow

in every moment
lies the power
to change eternity

how magnificent
the power of choice
to choose your reality
through your perception

how magical
the power of faith
to choose your reality
through your belief

how marvelous
the power of mind
to choose your reality
through your thoughts

the power of choice
we underestimate
the shifts
the changes
the miracles
that can happen
once we wholeheartedly
decide

how beautiful
the capacity we have
to change someone's life
to allow them
to change ours

the friendship that
shifted my perspective
became a container
that celebrated
existence
vulnerability
truth
that valued
a person whole

-sisterhood

the women in my life
have taught me
women are like trees

the unsung heros
rooted in the Earth
giving life to so many
weathering the storms
with ethereal grace

a yellow butterfly
came up to me

I'm exactly where
I'm supposed to be

-spirit signs

and it seems
that it all falls away
when all you have is now

the power of sound
to influence
    create
    heal
us and our realities
a cheat code
in this life
one already being used
through music
through television
through the words
we speak

take inventory
what are you taking in
how do you feel
what does your reality reveal

breathing deep
into my belly
into my womb
becoming one
with the infinite
source of all creation

the simple act
of mindful breathing
bearing witness
to your own existence
observing your thoughts
letting them pass
holding on to nothing
realizing you are not
these things

focusing on just being
                just breathing
reprogramming yourself
so subtly
clearing out chaos
bringing in stillness
with every breath
life beginning again

-meditation

yoga
body of God

meditation
breath of God

my body is a reminder
of my power
to create
to influence
to destroy
to resist

there is much freedom
in speaking
being
living
truth

kundalini
serpent energy
divine femininity
bursting forth
with every breath

gliding
up my spine
activating
awakening
strengthening
purifying
all my chakras

breaking through
stagnant energies
false identities
releasing worn out
versions of me

making room
for the goddess
being birthed within

goddess
archetypes
energies
beings
ancient
knowledge
Isis
Kali Ma
Venus
Oya
Hecate
Lilith
Parvati
Ma'at
Lakshmi
Hathor
Oshun
Sekhmet

guided me
through the darkest valleys
back toward the light of the Sun
helped me face my demons
embody my truth

I give gratitude for your presence
for this transformation
would not have been possible
without you

as I listen
as I trust
more

more
is entrusted
is told to me

proving
that this life is
a two-way street
a relationship of sorts
a balancing act
a reflection

as within
so without
as above
so below

you know a truth
by the way
it feels
in your bones

by the way
your third eye
opens wide

your heart gleams
your mind gets still
your senses get clearer

as if all of you
has been awakened
by the very moment

let your curiosity guide you
let your natural inclinations
lead the way forward

to think that your reality
is the only truth
is pure delusion

drop the judgement
others' journeys
are their journeys
yours is yours

there is not one path
                one way
to truth
don't let your arrogance
have you fooled

the ego is a prison
that paints itself
as a paradise
luring us in
with the false importance
of achievement
and preservation

injecting our minds
and clouding our souls
with the concept
of separateness
a concept that isolates us
into oblivion

you must never get confused
between who you are
and who you think
you should be

the ego
and the mind
can play tricks
don't be fooled

even when it makes
no sense at all
trust that it will

duality
a manmade concept
an attempt to add
meaning
logic
reasoning
to the ways of this world

the truth is
everything just is
we are all just being
there is no right
there is no wrong
merely existence

the vast range
of all that is
of all that we are
can consume us

leave us in a state
of utter confusion
or delusion
if we try too hard
to hold onto
what we thought
was true

what is real
what exists
what is truth
what escapes us
our minds
our perceptions
our fields of energy

this reality
could be deemed insanity
yet it all conjures itself up
in divine normality

if life is a movie
and I am the star
who is writing the script
who is directing the shots

for it is my subconscious
leading the way
choosing the stories
the lines to be said
the image to be captured
the scene to be played

how can so many
versions of me exist
with every person I've met
yet none of them be truly real

characters created
clouded by judgement
while soul essence
lives on
untouched
in the eternal moment

I am
a walking paradox
full of contradictions
of who you think I am
of who you think I've been
of who you think I could be

opinions
oppositions
that may not
make sense to you
yet it is somehow
in perfect harmony
and balance

these layers contain
all I've been
all I am
all I could be

I am
don't complicate it

the more I believe
in myself
in my abilities

mentally
physically
spiritually

the more my life aligns
into a space of divine
goodness and serendipity

giving myself grace
understanding
that I am bound
to make mistakes

that I am human
attempting to make sense
              to find meaning
on this journey

allowed to find freedom
from this matrix
allowed to find love
in this lifetime

I must
let love in
let love out
uncontrollably
unconditionally
and trust that
the greatest blessing
shall be allowing
love to flow

may love
soften my heart
like water
softens the rock

life goes on
and love comes again
maybe in a different form
but love comes again

let love
be your lighthouse
let it guide you
to new shores

as I lay between
the Earth
and the Sky
I realize one day
I will return to them both

for now
I enjoy my time
in the space in between

-thoughts while sunbathing

plant mama
a role
that has taught me
many life lessons
every plant
an individual being
its own needs
its own journey

teaching me
the importance
of honoring differences
each plant needing
its own balance
of light
of water
of love

teaching me
the necessity
in cutting off
the dead parts
for the wellbeing
of the whole

teaching me
the importance
of celebrating
signs of new life
of growth
no matter how small
no matter how slow

mother nature
my sanctuary
my healing center
my omnipresent nurturer

don't look
into the Sun
they say
but
I see God

-Ra

I found God
in the song of a bird
in the laugh of a child
in the warmth of the sun
in the kiss of a lover
in the flow of the water
in the perfume of a rose
in the sweetness of a mango
in the look in your eyes

noticing the moments
in between
the beauty that lies
just beneath the veil

why did we come here
to feel and be felt
to see and be seen
to express
to impress
our will
and manifest it
into reality
to experience this realm
to evolve into higher beings

be mindful in every moment
knowing in these moments
are where you build
or destroy yourself
bring yourself closer
to truth
or distract yourself
further into oblivion

this life is
a beautiful contradiction
a mirage of the full spectrum
  of consciousness
  of desires
  of possibilities

possibilities that hold no morality
only expression
only existence
only totality

creation
destruction
it is all one and the same

it all takes time
yet it doesn't
you see it is all
one eternal moment
stretching as wide
or as short
as we decide it to be

leave space
make room
for the universe
to do what it has to do

allow the river of life
to take what it takes
to bring what it brings
there is freedom in
not attaching yourself
to anything

life shows you
there is no finish line
just milestones you reach
and then
you keep going
reaching higher

that is the beauty of life
never-ending progression
                    transformation

always knowing
there is more
to look forward to
better to grow into

forgive yourself
forgive others
for those versions
of you
of them
no longer exist
they are only ghosts
haunting you

give yourself permission
to look and see
through new eyes
through the lens of now

teach
through being
let your life
be your legacy

thank God
for never giving up on me
even after
I'd given up on myself
a thousand times

I cannot imagine
where my life would be
without the kindness of strangers
angels on Earth

this has been
a season
of integration
and embodiment
of becoming one
with myself

free
free
free

free from
all I am
expected to be

free from
the anxiety inducing
what ifs
and controlling energy
that once seeped
out of me

free from
trying to be
perfect
right
in all that I do

free to
be seen
and heard
in all my
authentic glory

free to
feel the liberation
that comes from
living rooted
in truth and in love

I am bursting with joy
that I have finally arrived
at this place in time
at this state of mind

knowing in every ounce
of my bone
of my breath
who I truly am
who I always was
who I am destined to be

magician
without the hat

witch
without the broom

alchemist
without the gold

I've come dressed like
the new age Nefertiti
with all the power
and beauty
to shift the world

Saturn is returning
and so am I